# The Replacement Economy
# How do we get there?

Mark Burton

GreenDealManchester

http://greendealmanchester.wordpress.com/

Manchester: 2010

Version 2.2: 27 February 2010

The Replacement Economy: how do we get there?

Mark H Burton

Manchester 2010



ISBN 978-1-4457-7518-0

# The Replacement Economy: how do we get there?

## Contents

## Preface

We are living in an ecological emergency and an economic crisis. Yet despite there being plenty of recognition of the problems of emission-caused climate change, resource depletion, habitat and biodiversity destruction and an economic recession, there is no plan. Well there are some plans but either they won't deliver the change needed because they leave the fundamental causes untouched (e.g. public spending cuts and carbon trading), their scale is woefully inadequate to address the problem (e.g. renewable energy feed in tariffs, isolated energy efficiency measures) or they lack an adequate praxis - that is to say a combination of a theory of action and a practical strategy to go with it (e.g. transition towns, Green electoral strategies).

This pamphlet doesn't offer a solution to that conundrum but it brings together three contributions to what will have to become an ambitious but alternative strategy for real change in the way we all live.

They should be read in conjunction with **A Green Deal for the Manchester-Mersey Bioregion** published in 2009 and available in this series or at http://greendealmanchester.wordpress.com. That pamphlet sets out an approach to taking the necessary steps for meaningful change on what we call the bioregional scale. Its vision is bold, calling for urgent and drastic action that completely restructures the way we organise to produce and distribute the things we need to have worthwhile lives, and do this fairly and sustainably. It argues that because of the imperatives of reducing energy expenditure and (re)generating a real local economy it is at the Regional level that transformative green strategies can make the most sense. It also promotes the idea of a *replacement economy* to take the place of both the finance bubble economy and the economy of real production and distribution that is not only unsustainable but hurrying the ecosystem to destruction.

The three essays printed here complement that first pamphlet.

Both *Getting Started on the Economy* and *Sustainability Utopian and Scientific* start from the recognition that endless economic growth is not possible (and there is therefore some overlap in the early passages).

*Getting started on the Economy* also points to the incoherence of competition in the global economy as a national or regional economic strategy. It then goes on to set out some alternative principles for building the replacement economy and suggests priorities for activists to help bring them about. ***Sustainability Utopian and Scientific*** offers a constructive critique of what has become mainstream green economic thinking, using the model of Engels' famous critique of utopian socialism. The anti-growth lobby identifies the right problem but fails to fully excavate the roots of the growth fetish in the political economy of capitalism. And worse, the utopian proposals of groups like the New Economics Foundation "come with no analysis of how changes can be brought about- there is little or no theory of action, just a 'tell-and-hope' reformism".

*Concepts for Bioregional Development* is a glossary of concepts used in these papers which together try to integrate perspectives from ecological thought, together with those from politics and economics. It is an attempt to synthesise a new integrated vocabulary for the new economics of social and ecological justice.

Mark Burton

May 2010

# Getting started on the economy[1]

There is a striking consensus about the nature of the economic development that is needed in the UK. The main political parties, business, the unions and most economic commentators share two basic assumptions[2].

1. That economic growth must continue, year on year.
2. That success depends on being competitive in the global economy.

I am going to dispute those assumptions and then suggest some different ways of thinking about economic development before briefly suggesting some ways that we, activists can try to move in that direction[3]. The ideas presented here are not particularly original, but perhaps their juxtaposition is[4].

## Growth

Growth over the last 10 years in the UK has averaged 2.64% p.a. - an economy that *doubles* in size every 26 years[5]. The global economy is almost 5 times the size it was 50 years ago[6].

This has an environmental cost. Our ecological footprint in the UK is 5.3 hectares per person - that is to say we each depend on that area for our consumables, recreation, carbon sequestration and so on. But the available 'biocapacity' of the UK provides little more than half that (3.7) - a negative ecological debt[7]. As growth increases our ecological debt increases along with that of all the other countries. As the Global Footprint Network[8] puts it:

> *Today humanity uses the equivalent of 1.3 planets to provide the resources we use and absorb our waste. This means it now takes the Earth one year and four months to regenerate what we use in a year.*

*Moderate UN scenarios suggest that if current population and consumption trends continue, by the mid 2030s we will need the equivalent of two Earths to support us. And of course, we only have one.*

*Turning resources into waste faster than waste can be turned back into resources puts us in global ecological overshoot, depleting the very resources on which human life and biodiversity depend.*

Some have suggested that it is possible to decouple growth from material throughput - that is to make growth happen without corresponding growth in resource inputs (fuel, food, materials) and waste outputs (emissions of all sorts) - having our cake without getting obese. But the evidence, as reviewed by Tim Jackson, Economics Commissioner for the UK government's Sustainable Development Commission[9] is that only a *relative* reduction in throughput is feasible. The *absolute* level of resources needed and waste produced continues to rise. So the ecological overshoot or ecological debt just goes on getting worse.

This problem is brought into stark relief by two fatal challenges:

1. ***Peak energy***. Oil, gas, uranium and even coal are at or approaching the point at which the rate of exploitation of resources falls behind the rate of use. This means an energy crunch. We had a taste of this in 2008 with oil prices rising steeply. That was mostly a result of speculation, but this kind of volatility is likely to increase as the gap between exploitation and usage widens.

2) ***Climate change***: all the indications are that the situation is far worse than had been anticipated. Positive feedback effects ('non-linearities') magnify the impact of the rising carbon dioxide levels but they hadn't been properly understood and accounted (for example by the earlier Intergovernmental Panel on Climate Change reports) and hence government targets already too little and too late are now dramatically inadequate.

The first problem makes economic growth, reliant on its energy subsidy, implausible. The second problem makes it suicidal. In any case growth does not reliably produce wellbeing beyond a certain level (reached in the UK by the mid 1960s[10] although still to be reached in much of the majority world[11]). That is not its function anyway in terms of the overall political economy where growth like consumerism is a product of the logic of capital accumulation[12].

## International competitiveness

As recently as the 1970s the UK manufactured much of what it needed. Then we got 'globalisation' and manufacturing was mostly exported to countries with cheap labour. The globalization of trade is not new. Back in the 1890s cheap wheat imports from the USA and Russia were driving UK farmers (including my own great grandparents) off the land. As a child in the 1950s some of my toys were imported from China (well Hong Kong). So the idea of specialising in certain areas of wealth generation and not competing where other international regions had competitive advantage goes back as long as fossil hydrocarbons have been subsidising the economy, and to some degree before that.

But the twin barriers of peak energy and climate change put an end to this. It simply won't be possible to import food and manufactured goods from across the world at anything like the scale we have become used to. It is even questionable how much national trade there would be with less (and much costlier) energy available to move things.

The idea of a UK region being competitive in a global context makes good sense in the context of cheap energy-fed globalised capitalism where production goes after cheap resource imports, cheap labour and new markets. But sooner than you might think it will no longer work, and will no longer be relevant. So investments made on the basis of this assumption are likely to be poor ones.

## Alternative assumptions

So if we need to live on drastically reduced energy budgets we will need to adopt some new concepts to guide the development of prosperity. Here are some suggestions[13].

## *1) Endogenous development*[14].

Endogenous development means 'development from within', using the human and material resources to hand rather than relying on investment from outside. It means building up local, ecologically sustainable production and distribution for need in place of building development on captured wealth from elsewhere. This isn't just a case of bottom-up development - government has a role to play in facilitating it, just as it has always had with developments deemed to be national priorities[15]. Sources of investment for endogenous development could include

a) **Public Subscription** - this after all was how much of the 19th Century municipal heritage was funded, including some of the hospitals whose buildings are still in use. This has not been done much recently, but people do support charities, schools, community projects, so this is really an extension of the that practice.

b) **Municipal Green Investment Bonds** - issued by the council, or perhaps a body established through the City Region arrangements - allowing the combination of government funding, local government funding and income, and savings investment by local people. The bonds would offer safe investment and support development of sustainable economic activity - for example buying green belt land for local vegetable production, or enabling a more rapid insulation refit for the housing stock. Ultimately local pension funds might invest in these vehicles.

## *2) Trade subsidiarity (strategic localism)*

This means choosing carefully what to buy and sell beyond the local region. Only those things that cannot be sourced or produced locally should be brought in. There will still be some relationships with other parts of the world (just as there were before the age of hydrocarbon powered ships). These will involve necessary trade, sharing of knowledge and solidarity. In our relatively fortunate situation we have an ongoing responsibility to some producers as a result of the distortion of agriculture and other production over the years of colonial and postcolonial exploitation, to help such regions themselves to endogenously develop.

### *3) Bioregional scaling*

Endogenous development and trade subsidiarity mean we also have to think carefully about the size of a region that can be reasonably self-reliant in most things its population needs. A best guess would be what has been called a bioregion, or eco-region - often defined by the catchment of a river. An example is the area bounded by the Mersey watershed - Greater Manchester and Merseyside together with rural hinterland extending into the Pennines and parts of rural Lancashire and Cheshire. This would offer considerable diversity of ecologies and natural resources which will in turn have to be safeguarded and repaired to secure the sustenance for human settlement. Ultimately the bioregional scale will not be a policy choice but one made out of necessity. For now however we can make a positive choice to emphasise development within this scale.

An important related idea is the 'bioregional multiplier effect' - this is discussed quite well in *Bioregional Solutions: For Living on One Planet* by Pooran Desai and Sue Riddlestone[16]. If, for example we sourced 90% of our textiles from within the bioregion ( wool, flax, hemp, nettles, cellulose/rayon) then this would mean jobs locally in agriculture, manufactures (retting, carding, spinning, weaving, dyeing, finishing etc etc - also making the new equipment needed for extraction of plant fibres), distribution. This would mean more money spent locally which given other bioregionally based production (food, timber, etc) would mean the support of a more closed loop economy both in materials and circulating money. Contrast this with Primark, where the money spent goes straight out of the region to the Spanish owners, and the maquiladora[17] capitalists, enabling the exploitation of workers overseas, not to mention the environmental costs of cotton production alone. However, that really does all need tying back to the critique of economic growth and capital accumulation. The bioregional multiplier needs careful distinction from the Keynesian multiplier which simply feeds indiscriminate economic growth - a problem with the NEF New Green Deal approach that might be characterised as 'mitigated business as usual'.

### *4) A new model of community*

Ultimately this new world of low energy and local self reliance means a new approach to community life, one that could offer a solution to many of our present social ills. It means moving towards a way of living based on common interests, sharing and conviviality in place of the sad spectacle of pointless and alienated consumption and competition. This model of community emphasises mutuality and cooperation[18] - fair exchange rather than the unequal exchange and exploitation that is the hidden side of the current model. A discussion paper on inclusive and sustainable communities by John O'Brien and David Towell gives an interesting angle on this[19].

### *5) Democratic decision making.*

One problem with the present model is that the people most affected - workers, consumers, have little influence over things like investments, product development, the location and subsidy of industry and other types of production, and so on. Of course the market is supposed to do this instead, but the very existence of the term 'market failure' indicates how naïve that idea is. The anarchy of the market has to be consciously countered by deliberative decision making. A participatory economy is what we are after here[20].

### *6) A careful analysis of resource realities in relation to organisational and economic options.*

This means a brave openness to evidence. Just because we like mutuality and small scale solutions doesn't mean that they are always the most appropriate. Often they are, but, for example, to make the big changes that are necessary in the energy infrastructure means both State intervention and the use of existing sources of capital to provide a big enough mobilisation of the necessary resources[21] - for example to build and distribute tidal-based energy or that from offshore wind farms, or deep geothermal energy. It is the orthodoxies of growth in the global market that are dogmatic and closed to the evidence - we don't have to emulate them. We need therefore to select among the following economic and organisational models, depending on the scale and nature of the problem –

**Community-based enterprise**: an interesting model from recent history is the Chinese township and village enterprise model that was very successful in promoting modest community level prosperity prior to the 'get rich' policy that led to their demise along with the breakneck growth of the Chinese economy.

**Private enterprise**: not in the meaning of the right wing ideologues who use this term to mean big business, but non-capitalist small firms (i.e. those that do not produce a surplus that is then used to create more surplus). There are many of these companies, for example in the building trade and farming.

**Co-operatives**: there are very viable models of this mode – for example the Co-operative movement in the UK, the Industrial Common Ownership firms like John Lewis (pity they are consumerist retail-focussed), and the Mondragon industrial cooperatives in northern Spain.

**The State**: remember that the propaganda about inefficiency of the State as proprietor was very much exaggerated, and privatisation of state enterprise has simply increased capital accumulation, the motor of growth – the problem we are trying to fix here. And at the local level there is a role for municipal enterprise – rather than depending on the airport our councils could be encouraged to invest in the replacement economy. And the State has a clear role to play in the context of market failure.

**The corporate sector**: as indicated above, since the wealth lies in this sector, we have to work with it in some areas since there is otherwise insufficient to invest, particularly in infrastructure projects necessary if the replacement economy is to rise above a subsistence level.

The implications of the end of economic growth and global competitiveness are profound and mean nothing less than a third industrial revolution, with an emphasis on production and distribution for need. It means the end of capital accumulation as the driver of the economy but it is still unclear what will take its place. The real challenge will be to scale down economic activity without abandoning large sections of the population to deprivation on a scale that will make the social conditions of the first industrial revolution look like a tea party[22].

So far so easy - we know what's wrong and we've some idea of what is needed, but here is the difficult bit: how do we get going on this agenda? How can we bring about the changes needed here in Britain's North West? Where do we start? Who do we engage? What could go wrong?

Real change is only likely to come through shocks to the system. The most likely ones are in terms of food and fuel scarcity due to rising oil costs and climactic change. New Economics Foundation calculate that the UK has such little food storage capacity, as a result of combined import dependency and just in time distribution approaches, that we are no more than "Nine Meals from Anarchy[23]". This graphically illustrates the precariousness of our consumerist paradise.

Here are some initial thoughts - in the form of action guidelines:

1) **Identify the nodes from which the replacement economy can grow.** Find the projects, initiatives that can be scaled up when the opportunity arises. Some examples are things like producer co-ops and community supported agriculture. But also look beyond the obvious green and 'alternative society[24]' initiatives - what is happening in places like Newton Heath or Abbey Hey[25]? What are small (and larger) businesses doing, especially those that are not tied to the logic of capital accumulation/growth? I'm not so far convinced by the various green pound schemes as transformationally potent[26] but maybe they can make the necessary step change and keep some resources within a purely exchange-based system rather than that linked to capital accumulation and growth.

2) **Focus on building resilience through initiatives.** The wider system will need these elements once the inevitable shocks to the economy, the climate, food and warmth, happen. The coordinating bodies (councils, government organisations, Qangos[27], police etc.) have some interest in shock-proofing the population and projects that serve this function can attract resources (public, private, joint).

3) **Lever system resources into the new economy.** The above strategy is one example of levering resources from the old economy into the new replacement economy. In the above example, resources that build resilience also serve the function of establishing non-accumulative enterprise - that is to say the 'system resources' can be levered into an incipient economy that is not based on growth for growth's sake, but on meeting human need. There must be other examples of ways to do this - but the trick, in an era of reducing government spending will be to find resource streams outside the State (and its creatures) to lever into the replacement economy. The two examples given in the above discussion on endogenous development would also be consistent with this idea.

4) **Join in campaigns for local economic initiatives and against business as usual ones.** An example is the campaign against Tesco's colonisation of the local retail economy. And while eco-consumerism is a change tool of strictly limited scope in real transformative change there is no excuse for buying from any supermarket other than the Co-op - why pay your money to a sector that sucks money and jobs out of the local economy and destroys local diversity? Similarly support campaigns to share the work around - maximising employment and reducing income inequalities. Also of great importance is to support campaigns against the privatisation of what remains of public and socially owned resources: this commodification of the public sphere is a key part of Capital's strategy for endless growth, a response to the internal contradictions of the capitalist system[28].

5) **Take part in the debate.** For example challenge orthodox, ***Business as Usual*** thinking in the many consultations, through the press, at meetings. It doesn't matter that we don't have all the answers - a start is to keep on pointing out the nudity of the emperor, and the bankruptcy of the empire.

The ideas offered here are not complete and require further work. Do contribute to the debate through the website http://greendealmanchester.wordpress.com/ or by email contactgdm@googlemail.com

Mark Burton

February 2010, updated May 2010, September 2010.

# Sustainability: Utopian and Scientific

## Introduction

To make the move to a sustainable future where people are no longer threatened by an ecological catastrophe will require a number of things - above all a strong and broad movement with effective and intelligent leadership and an accurate understanding of the current problems and how they can be overcome. Sadly, only some parts of this constellation of forces are in place today. In particular the green movement is not an effective political and social movement and the left is still in disarray, largely concerned with defensive politics and harking back to a world long gone.

As for ideas and analysis of the situation and what needs to be done, some powerful critiques[29] of the current economic orthodoxies have recently appeared that set out an alternative way in which the wellbeing and prosperity of the population can be achieved and maintained. However, these contributions are insufficient since they do not provide a sufficiently profound diagnosis of the causes of the problem. Without such a diagnosis there can be no convincing prescription for a remedy. But the situation is even worse than that. There is also no convincing approach to obtaining the necessary changes.

The situation is not unlike that which Frederick Engels faced in the 1870s when he wrote "Socialism, Utopian and Scientific"[30]. Engels respected the utopian socialists Saint-Simon, Fourier and Owen for their identification of the dire effects of the super-exploitative capitalist system as its growth gained speed in the first half of the 19th century. But he pointed out that they had not understood the generative mechanisms by which it dominated society and caused these dire consequences for working people. Nor had they any convincing praxis - that is to say they neither had a theory of how its domination might be ended nor a programme for hastening that end. He counterposed *scientific socialism* - that is socialism that has an understanding of the causes of class dominance and the role of the working class in their own emancipation - with *utopian socialism* which named the problem, proposed utopian alternatives, but was idealist in the sense that it thought it would be enough to convince enough people of the rightness of the alternative way. It will be argued here that an analogous situation exists today with regard to the agenda of sustainability and specifically with the idea that economic growth is not sustainable.

There is still a striking consensus about the nature of the economic development that is needed, not just in the UK but on a global scale. The main political parties, business, the unions, the international agencies, the so-called economists and the pundits in the media all assume that economic growth must continue, year on year.

First we need to look at the argument against this.

## The problem with economic Growth[31]

Growth over the last 10 years in the UK has averaged 2.64% p.a. - an economy that *doubles* in size every 26 years[32]. The global economy is almost 5 times the size it was 50 years ago[33]. It is generally assumed that around 3% growth per annum is healthy for an economy.

Such growth has an environmental cost. The ecological footprint of the UK is 5.3 hectares per person - that is to say we each depend on that area for our consumables, recreation, carbon sequestration and so on. But the available 'biocapacity' of the UK provides little more than half that (3.7) - a negative ecological debt[34]. As growth increases our ecological debt increases along with that of all the other countries. As the Global Footprint Network puts it:

> *Today humanity uses the equivalent of 1.3 planets to provide the resources we use and absorb our waste. This means it now takes the Earth one year and four months to regenerate what we use in a year.*
>
> *Moderate UN scenarios suggest that if current population and consumption trends continue, by the mid 2030s we will need the equivalent of two Earths to support us. And of course, we only have one.*

*Turning resources into waste faster than waste can be turned back into resources puts us in global ecological overshoot, depleting the very resources on which human life and biodiversity depend.* [35]

Some have suggested that it is possible to decouple growth from material throughput - that is to make growth happen without corresponding growth in resource inputs (fuel, food, materials) and waste outputs (emissions of all sorts) - having our cake without getting obese. But the evidence, as reviewed by Tim Jackson, Economics Commissioner for the UK government's Sustainable Development Commission[36] is that only a *relative* reduction in throughput is feasible. The *absolute* level of resources needed and waste produced continues to rise. So the ecological overshoot or ecological debt just goes on getting worse.

This problem is brought into stark relief by two fatal challenges:

> ***Peak energy***. Oil, gas, uranium and even coal are at or approaching the point at which the rate of exploitation of resources falls behind the rate of use. This means an energy crunch. We had a taste of this in 2008 with oil prices rising steeply. That was mostly a result of speculation, but this kind of volatility is likely to increase as the gap between exploitation and usage widens.
>
> ***Climate change***: all the indications are that the situation is far worse than had been anticipated. Positive feedback effects ('non-linearities') magnify the impact of the rising carbon dioxide levels but they hadn't been properly understood and accounted (for example by the earlier International Panel on Climate Change reports) and hence government targets, already too little and too late, now appear to be dramatically inadequate.

The first problem makes economic growth, reliant on its energy subsidy, implausible. The second problem makes it suicidal.

## Utopian sustainability

We can refer to two sources as representative of utopian sustainability. Firstly, the work of the New Economics Foundation (NEF), for example the New Green Deal paper published in 2008[37] and the work on alternative indicators of wellbeing to Gross Domestic product (GDP)[38]. Secondly, work by the Sustainable Development Commission (SDC), for example the critique of economic growth cited above. However, while critical of these efforts it is important to be very clear that they are fine so far as they go. More, they are a vital source for a 'scientific' approach to sustainability despite their utopian, or should we say Fabian[39], flavour.

The problem then is that although they present sound critiques of the effects, they offer no analysis of the systemic causes. Moreover their utopian proposals come with no analysis of how changes can be brought about[40]- there is little or no theory of action, just a 'tell-and-hope' reformism.

## Roots of the growth fetish

What we can call the growth fetish has multiple roots. These can be divided into the *ideological*, the *practical* and the *systemic*.

Firstly, a belief in the inevitability and necessity of growth seems like common sense. The idea of progress, of living better than our parents did is ingrained in our culture. As noted above, hardly anyone questions this - it is the current currency of political and economic discourse, both for those within the system and for many of those critical of it. But, common sense is not the same thing as good sense[41]. It reflects the dominant interests in the social system, and in this case, as we will see, the ideology reflects and supports the interests of Capital[42] - the growth fetish is *hegemonic*.

Secondly, growth has a practical appeal in the context of responding to social ills. Where the cake is growing it seems not to matter if people's shares are unequal, so long as they are all growing. This is actually illusory on two counts. Firstly, there is evidence (collated by NEF among others) that since the mid 1970s economic growth has not been associated with rises in life-satisfaction[43]. Secondly, this model of an increasing but unequally shared cake is flawed as a recipe for societal wellbeing: there is persuasive evidence that more unequal societies have a greater level of social ills, not just for the poor but for all strata[44]. Moreover, an unequally divided cake that grows becomes means an accentuation of the inequalities in absolute terms. Flawed it may be but this supposed practical root of the growth fetish has an extraordinary appeal - maybe because it seems to postpone or even avoid the need for more profound, and difficult, social reform. It therefore adds to the ideological support for the growth fetish.

## *Systemic causes of the addiction to growth*

The root cause of the growth fetish, however, does not lie in the ideological realm but rather is to be found in the inherent and defining feature of capitalism, the dominant economic system under and within which the majority of the earth's population now lives - an economic and social system that for some 200 years has efficiently created an explosion in production, access to goods and commodities, technological sophistication, population, longevity and knowledge. The motor for this has been capital, something that within this system has the propensity to increase[45]. That increase in capital is based fundamentally on exploitation - of workers, consumers and natural resources.

Capitalism, then is first and foremost a system that reproduces capital, that is to say it accumulates capital. To do this every social process is commodified: exchange, production, distribution, investment - previously conducted through media other than markets. And no social transaction is exempt from this process of commodification. To endlessly accumulate capital it is necessary to extract profit. This is done at various points in the system, and most obviously in the theft of surplus value from workers and the unequal exchange between the core areas of the system and the primary resource producing areas. Without unequal exchange capitalism cannot work.

Capitalism establishes institutions to support itself, the State with its legal and governmental system, the educational system, the welfare systems, and the armed forces. When unequal exchange is threatened, the legal and military systems are brought into action.

Capitalism as a system that reproduces capital must ever expand, finding new markets, new cheaper workforces, and new sources of raw materials, new products and new means of production. This is because the reproduction of capital means that there is always an oversupply. This means that new investment opportunities are continually sought. The oversupply problem has been a major contributor to the historical cycles in the world economy. Currently this is compounded by excess productive capacity and the suppression of wages since the late 70s - hence the extension of credit. Capitalism then tends toward crisis.

Capital, then, has to grow - that is the condition for its survival. It is this inexorable and inherent dynamic of capital accumulation that causes the growth fetish, the addiction to growth. Because there are powerful interests linked to this source of growth, telling the facts about the sustainability of economic growth will have little or no impact. The system simply cannot learn another way, it would be like suggesting that human beings should not drink water and the calls for sustainable growth are like saying 'well let them drink tea instead'.

It is the failure of the 'utopian' advocates of sustainability to properly identify the logic of capital accumulation as the root cause of the growth fetish that marks their distance from an adequate 'scientific' understanding of the nature of the problem and its resolution. In that sense they stand in a similar place as the C19th utopian socialists, incapable of doing more than calling to people of good will in the hope that their ideas will - against all the evidence - be taken up by a system that is fundamentally opposed to them - that knows no other way than capital accumulation and the associated economic growth.

## Scientific socialism

Now this term 'scientific', used by Engels in his famous pamphlet needs some explanation and justification. Engels explained the term as follows:

*These two great discoveries, the materialistic conception of history and the revelation of the secret of capitalistic production through surplus-value, we owe to Marx. With these discoveries Socialism became a science. The next thing was to work out its details and relations*[46].

Engels is pointing here to the systematic and evidence-based revelation of the underlying, historical causes of the features of the economic and social system. Socialism was the desirable state and he and Marx never lost the humanist, ethical impulse that inspired their work t that end, but ethical direction was not enough there had to be a proper grounding. As he indicates, this was work in progress, never finished by him and Marx, either in terms of the full analysis of the system or in terms of what the socialist alternative would look like[47].

The analogy with natural science is helpful, so far as it goes:-

*Active social forces work exactly like natural forces; blindly, forcibly, destructively, so long as we do not understand and reckon with them. But once we understand them, when once we grasp their action, their direction, their effects, it depends only upon ourselves to subject them more and more to our own will, and by means of them to reach their own ends. And this holds especially of the mighty productive forces of today. As long as we obstinately refuse to understand the nature and the character of these social means of action - and this understanding goes against the grain of the capitalist mode of production and its defenders - so long these forces are at work in spite of us, in opposition to us, so long they master us...*[48]

Engels is not suggesting that social forces are exactly like physical forces (he alludes to the ideological component in the last sentence), but he is pointing out that attempts at reform that take no account of their workings will be doomed to failure.

For Marx and Engels two key ideas made the connection between a scientific political economy as explanation of capitalist exploitation and the programme of the struggle for socialism: contradictions and class struggle[49].

### *Contradictions*

The complex system that is capitalism, being composed of different elements in motion, requiring simultaneous coordination but pulling in different directions, creates internal contradictions that force it into recurrent crises. Marx and Engels pointed to the contradiction between forces of production and relations of production - putting large groups of workers together meant creating new social relations, a new social force, the proletariat that by its concentration was able to organise together. Similarly the need to educate sections of the labour force also led to proletariat becoming more self-aware, more able to diagnose what was wrong with the world and to provide counter-system information, and persuasion. They also showed how the expansion of production contradicted the impoverishment of working people leading to repeated crises of oversupply and underconsumption, leading to the cycle of boom and bust (in Engels' day about every ten years). It was through its contradictions that the old order would be ended, although these would not be enough on their own without the key social movement of the working class.

### *Struggle and the movement*

Engels and Marx saw the struggle for socialism as the struggle of classes; that is as the struggle between groupings with contradictory interests, defined by their position within the system of capitalist production and capital accumulation. Capitalism would fall through the increasing power of the proletariat, itself created by capitalism (another contradiction) that would eventually overthrow the bourgeois order, either through revolution or through the ballot box.

## Scientific sustainability

What does this analogy with scientific socialism tell us about the process of achieving sustainability in a system that is even more dominated by the power of Capital than was the case in the C19th? An answer will be attempted, in outline here, in relation to the two key Marxist concepts of Contradiction and Struggle.

## *Contradictions and Crisis*

Capitalism, throughout its existence has been faced with repeated crises resulting from the internal contradictions it generates. Time and time again has it overcome these contradictions, showing a strategic flexibility that Marx and Engels cold not have imagined. These crises have largely been crises in capital accumulation driven by the falling rate of profit, the saturation of markets, the successful struggles of workers and other 'subaltern' populations, and the excessive productive capacity of the system. Each time 'fixes' have been found, technological, social, military, political, and financial, sometimes applied separately and sometimes together. Without going into a detailed analysis of these fixes, the following can be identified as particularly significant:

- $£€¥ Employment of new, cheap forms of energy (the energy subsidies).
- $£€¥ Development of new technologies for production, distribution or as commodity lines to sell.
- $£€¥ Importation of cheaper labour or outsourcing of production to sites with cheaper labour.
- $£€¥ Use of internationally distributed operations to play one currency against another and evade taxation.
- $£€¥ Creation of and expansion into new markets.
- $£€¥ The use of State power to provide subsidies (e.g. education and training for the workforce, health and welfare, infrastructure whether canals or satellite communications).
- $£€¥ The use of State power to subdue internal or external threats to capital accumulation by legislation, force or economic sanctions and incentives.
- $£€¥ The turning of areas of social life and nature into commodities (e.g. urban space, water, beaches, folk music,

mutual aid and so on) that can be traded or the return of such areas to the market (e.g. the privatisation of public services) and hence as nodes of capital accumulation and the transfer of public assets into private hands.

- $£€¥ The formation of cartels, whether as commercial trusts or through the legitimised international policy instruments of the World trade Organisation, IMF, World Bank, European Union, NAFTA and so on.
- $£€¥ Financialisation - the hyper-development of credit and debt into generators of capital for example through gambling on stocks, speculation and the invention of complex financial instruments.

The most recent phase of capitalist expansion, the neoliberal period, has been characterised by the deployment of all these elements in concert. As a result the capitalist model until very recently seemed unassailable. Yet as the present situation clearly demonstrates, the contradictions are coming home to roost again. And while up to now it has been the internal contradictions of capital that have created crises, now there are both internal contradictions and contradictions between the capitalist forces of production and the natural environment on which they depend (the contradiction between production economy and earth economy). So at this moment the world is faced with a set of interlocked crises - the financial crash and recession, the food crisis, the energy crisis, the water crisis, climate change, and the accompanying legitimation crises that take differing forms in different global locations and in different social sectors.

It is these contradictions and their resultant crises that provide the key to a transition to a different sustainable system. We do not know the precise point at which the contradictions will prove fatal for capital accumulation. Nor do we know how bloody that end will be. But what is now beyond doubt is that capitalism, at least in its totalising dominant viral expansionist mode will end through a combination of internal and external contradictions that can not be fixed. It is possible, indeed likely, that a restricted capitalism will continue in certain sectors, but it can not continue to be the one principle that structures the whole economy and therefore (in the last analysis) all social arrangements.

However, these contradictions and crises will not just end unsustainable capitalist growth by themselves; this depends on there being a protagonist - the midwife of history.

## *Struggle and social movements*

For Marx and Engels the protagonist, the midwife of history was to be the proletariat, the class consisting of those forced by (socially constructed) economic realities to sell their labour power to Capital. But more than a century later that protagonist no longer exists in the same form. To be sure global Capital has its proletariat, concentrated in the factories of China, the maquiladoras of Mexico, the polytunnels of Murcia, and these sectors will continue to struggle against their exploiters. Yet while both wings of he socialist movement, Leninist and social democrat were founded in and of the proletariat as collective subject of transition to a new world, in none of the transformative C20th revolutions was the proletariat the decisive protagonist (although they played their part in each). From the Mexican revolution through the Russian, Chinese, Cuban, Algerian and Vietnamese revolutions in no case was it the proletarian mass power that led the transformation. This was only the case in the failed revolutions of the metropolitan countries. Only in the reformist case of mitigated capitalism, best seen in Scandinavia, could it be said that the proletarian movement was the hegemonic component. And today in Latin America the progressive protagonists in Venezuela, Bolivia, Ecuador and elsewhere are again to be found in other sectors, chiefly in the alliance between sectors(indigenous communities, the urban masses of the barrios, the landless peasants) whose exclusion has been more profound even than that of the proletariat (who after all are within the system of production and reproduction of Capital) and other unorthodox elements such as progressive clergy and sections of the military.

However, the most profound areas of contradiction at present, the final limits of the capitalist mode of production (and reproduction), are to be found in the twin areas of climate change and peak energy. So for anyone concerned with sustainability as a goal, having analysed why the system is unsustainable - growth based on capital accumulation - must identify a protagonist adequate to the challenge. And having identified that protagonist it is necessary to nurture it, just as Marx and Engels did with the embryonic proletarian movement.

Who is that protagonist, that collective subject, that midwife of history at the start of the C21st? For this it is helpful to turn to the insights of Antonio Gramsci, the founder of the Italian communist party who was the first to systematically apply Marxist analysis to the more complex order of capitalism in a liberal democratic context[50]. This is not to say that Gramsci's context was the same as ours today - further insights will be necessary. However his key contribution was the analysis of the role of ideas in collective action - essentially the roles of ideology and the nature of leadership in a mass movement. Gramsci emphasised how a bloc of interests can come together under a leadership that can offer a unifying ideology. That ideology will not be total - different interest groups will be attracted by different facets of it and will pick and mix elements. The ideology will hold the movement together and the leadership will adapt it to circumstances. For Gramsci that leadership is composed of organic intellectuals - intellectuals who serve not the dominant system but the movement, and are embedded within it, learning their craft within the movement. He also identifies the collective nature of the leadership of a social movement - in his case that was the Party - with the metaphor of the Modern Prince - Machiavelli's statesman who showed adaptability, firmness, cunning and forethought, transformed into an ethical subject that coordinated the actions of the movement. Gramsci's notions then are quite some way from those of the Leninists who have dominated the radical left with notions of vanguard. They are also miles away from both the cynical electoral/media/power nexus politics of what is left of the social democratic movement, or the self-indulgent and ineffectual anarchism that pervades the Green movement (when it isn't being Fabian). A reading of Gramsci's politics for today (for we want to use his ideas today not in their actual context of the 1920s) is that of the progressive coalition united in diversity with an adaptive core ideology that is inclusive not exclusive for all those that want to end the unsustainable system of capitalism - planetary consumption.

Concretely this means that the protagonist has to be the broad social movement of green and left activists, trade unionists, food activists, minority rights, social and trade justice activists and internationalists. But this movement has still to be built, using local, national and international struggles as the focus, with a shared programme for transformation from capitalism to a sustainable socialist alternative. It will be essential to peel off layers of those who up to now have seen their fate as linked to capitalism, whether they are leaders who have developed their cities through Capital-funded regeneration, legislators who have tried to ameliorate capitalism through regulation and limited redistributive policies, consumers who are waking up to the con of unsustainable consumption, state officials who have until now seen their role as administering the policy recipes of neoliberal capitalism and academics who have had enough of adapting their thought, teaching and research to the dictates of the god of endless consumption and growth, accountants who now get their sums right and find they just don't add up.

The form, programme, strategy, and tactics - the leadership- of such a movement have yet to emerge but without it there is no chance of the kind of sustainable future that the utopian advocates of sustainability have promoted. They have taken us so far but now is the time to get scientific - in the best Marxian sense of the word - to understand profoundly and to act.

## *Internationalism and localism*

Capitalism is a global system. Like the life of an animal it exists at the micro (workplace, shop, household - molecular and cellular) level, at the meso (firm, organ) level and at the macro level (conglomerate, industry, economy State - whole animal) as well as existing over time from generation to generation and through nested cycles of energy transactions, production, consumption, reproduction. Everywhere you look you see it. Everywhere you turn it is there before you. More than that it is you - in your food, your thoughts, your emotions and the systems that tie these together. Around you and in you and beyond you.

This means that it has to be fought in many places at once - locally, nationally, globally, through local projects, conversations, struggles, alliances and through actions that tie together across territories and globally. While we take the view that the bioregional level is particularly important for interventions that prefigure (another Gramscian reference) a better way of organising society, this is not to deny the importance of making alliances at other levels. It is not enough to think globally - act locally. It is necessary to act and think both locally and globally - just like Capital does.

## *Reform and revolution*

Much of what has been written above will sound revolutionary and unremittingly oppositional. The system is dominant but its dominance is not complete. Those working within its institutions are not its unthinking servants, and their actions are not entirely constrained and determined by Capital. There are various spaces where Capital has been tamed - for example within the institutions of the local state, or where alternative social and even economic modes are in play, if only partially - like cooperatives and some non-government and community organisations. Working for transformation, being part of the new to-be-hegemonic social movement requires a strategy of simultaneous insider - outsider tactics. Where a city administration is working on a climate change action plan, for example, it is essential both to work with them to develop the plan and to work outside to keep up the pressure for real and radical action. Indeed we should aim for proposals that cannot be delivered under capitalism as part of a broader strategy of weakening the very causes of unsustainable economic activity, both to change the system but also because such proposals are the right thing to support - in this case the only way to deliver carbon reductions of sufficient size to avert catastrophic warming. As an infamous politician would say - There Is No Alternative[51].

An example of such a transitional demand[52] could be the work on macroeconomic policy in Tim Jackson's SDS report[53] – not that it will have been conceived in these terms – the intention seems to have been more naïvely Fabian in style. He sets out the problem to be tackled like this:

> *.... when demand falls, revenues to firms are reduced and this leads to job losses and reduced investment. Reduced investment leads to a lower capital stock which, together with a lower labour input, in turn reduces the productive capability of the economy. Output falls and with less money in the economy, public revenues also fall, debt is more difficult to service and the system has a tendency to become unstable.*
>
> *But does it have to work like this? Is it possible to configure the conventional macro-economic variables in such a way as to reduce the imperative for growth and yet maintain economic stability? One potential avenue of exploration is to attempt a stabilisation of economic output by altering the role or relative importance of key variables (such as consumption, investment, public spending and so on) within the basic macro-economic model.*[54]

Jackson explores the parameters for a national economy that does not depend on economic growth are explored drawing on the Canadian scenarios of Peter Victor[55]. Jackson concludes that it is possible to have an economy with low growth/resource throughput with both unemployment and poverty halved. This depends in part on reducing working hours. However, greenhouse gas emissions on this model only reduce slowly. Jackson himself adds a number of cautions.

> *These conditions will still include a strong requirement for economic stability. Or perhaps 'resilience' would be a better word for what is required here. A sustainable economy must be capable of resisting the exogenous shocks and avoid the internal contradictions which have caused chaos in the last year.*
>
> *But the requirement for resilience will need to be augmented by conditions that address distributional equity, impose sustainable levels of resource throughput, and provide for the protection of critical natural capital.*
>
> *In operational terms, this new macro-economy will require enhanced investment in public infrastructures, in sustainable technologies and in*

*ecosystem maintenance. It is likely to demand a different balance between public and private goods. It will require us to reframe our concepts of productivity and profitability. Above all, a new macro-economics for sustainability will be ecologically and socially literate, ending the folly of separating economy from society and environment.*

But in outlining these conditions hasn't Jackson identified enough reasons why a system built on capital accumulation cannot deliver this?

Yet the need to understand how to manage a macro-economy in a different way is a real need for a transitional strategy. The Russian, Chinese and Cuban revolutions all faced major challenges in this regard with resulting oscillations in economic policy. An understanding of how to manage the capitalist economy into something else is clearly required by strategists of scientific sustainability: without it the likelihood is of a nightmare scenario of rising civil strife, rising poverty and political instability with the key need to rapidly move to a low carbon future severely compromised.

## Conclusion

*Political change comes from leadership and popular mobilisation. And you need both of them*[56]*.*

It has been argued that the valuable work done by bodies such as the NEF and SDS on the zero growth sustainable economy suffer from a kind of Utopianism. That is to say they do not fully take account of the systemic causes of the growth fetish. Nor do they identify what conditions could bring about its replacement, and as such they are bereft of political strategy. It is argued that the root cause of the growth addiction is the system of capitalism with its central motor of capital accumulation. Moreover it is argued that the internal and increasingly the external contradictions of that system will push it into a terminal crisis. However, that crisis will not simply arrive and usher in a new era of sanity. It will require a broad social movement, broader than any we have seen yet, with an intelligent and strategic leadership. That leadership will not be based in a traditional political party but in a network of activist thinkers who share a common vision and agreement on the main dimensions of strategy. That movement and that leadership will gather strength in the months and years to come, and its nature will change over time, in response to changing conditions. But it is the duty of everyone who wants a sustainable and equitable future to build that movement and that leadership and to do that with unprecedented rapidity, for there is no time to lose.

Mark Burton

July 2009

http://greendealmanchester.wordpress.com

# Concepts for bioregional development

*Bioregion, Bubble, Capacitation, Capital, Carrying capacity, City Region, Contradiction, Crash, Crisis, Drawdown, Edge, Endogenous development, Energy austerity, Energy descent, Energy subsidy, Fiscal stimulus, Food security, Green Deal, Green New Deal, Keynesianism, Marxism, Peak Energy, Permaculture, Resilience, Shock proofing, Strategic localism, Trade subsidiarity, Transition, Watershed*

## Bioregion

The missing element from much current work on transition to a low energy economy. A natural region, based on landforms and ecosystems rather than arbitrary political boundaries (although they do sometimes coincide). Often bounded by hills and mountains, coasts, rivers or defined by river catchment systems. A distinction is sometimes made between geo-regions and eco-regions but both are types of bioregion. Bioregions of different scale are nested within one another and they also overlap.

*"Archaeology records a series of civilisations that rose and fell as they depleted their bioregional resource base."* David Holmgren

See http://greendealmanchester.wordpress.com/the-manchester-bioregion/

http://blog.permacultureglobalreport.com/2008/03/find-your-life-place.html

Key text Sale, K (1985) Dwellers in the Land, San Francisco (USA): Sierra Club.

## Bubble

Speculative growth in financial assets that outstrips the value that can be sustained by a more fundamental measure. So the recent phase of financialisation of the economy has meant the inflation of property values and that of stock and commodity derivatives to a degree that a crash in valuation was inevitable. It is also arguable that the so called real economy that underpinned the financial economy is itself a bubble dependent on temporary support from finite energy subsidies. Again values will crash when they can no longer be sustained, or example as a result of the escalating cost of transport.

See

Gowan, P. (2009) Crisis in the Heartland: Consequences of the New Wall Street System New Left Review 55, http://www.newleftreview.org/?page=article&view=2759

David Harvey interview *Exploring the logic of capital*: http://www.socialistreview.org.uk/article.php?articlenumber=10801

Carlota Pérez, C. (2009) *Technological roots and structural implications of the double bubble at the turn of the Century* http://www-cfap.jbs.cam.ac.uk/publications/files/WP31.pdf.

## Capacitation

Term literally translated from the Spanish and Portuguese. However in English it does not have a ready meaning and is sometimes wrongly translated as 'training'. It means something more akin to the combination of training and development of appropriate and productive methods together with the support structures needed to make them feasible. It implies an investment in human capital, not just in knowledge and skills but also in the social relations and social supports necessary for the realisation of the benefit from training and education[57].

See Carmen, R (2000) *A Future for the Excluded: Job Creation and Income Generation by the Poor - Clodomir Santos De Morais and the Organizational Workshop*. London: Zed Books.

## Capital

We use the word with a capital 'C' to indicate the subsystem of capital in economic terms together with the actions, strategy, ideology of those who work to increase the accumulation of capital - its production and reproduction and expansion. These people were initially the classical industrial capitalists of the 19th Century, but over the last 100 years the function has been to greater or lesser extent become systemic in nature, with the development of professions such as accountancy and the establishment of bodies such as pension funds and corporate bonds that function objectively as the capitalist.

See Harvey, D (2006) **Limits to Capital**, London, Verso.

http://davidharvey.org/

The term capital is also used in accounting in a more restricted sense to mean non-recurrent and usually large sums of money, typically used for buildings and other plant. This meaning, depending on the system in which it is utilised, is close to the Marxist notion of fixed capital.

Human capital is used to describe the acquired capacities of a population or group. Social capital (Bourdieu, Putnam - who use the term in rather different ways) refers to the supportive, solidarity-forging interrelations among the members of that population, respectively. See Kagan, C et al Community Activism, Participation and Social Capital on a Peripheral Housing Estate
http://www.compsy.org.uk/bergenpaper_social_capital.pdf

## Carrying capacity

*In ecological terms, the carrying capacity of an ecosystem is the size of the population or community that can be supported indefinitely upon the available resources and services of that ecosystem. Living within the limits of an ecosystem depends on three factors:*

1. *the amount of resources available in the ecosystem;*
2. *the size of the population or community; and*
3. *the amount of resources each individual within the community is consuming.*

From the Encyclopaedia of sustainable development
http://www.ace.mmu.ac.uk/esd/menu.html
http://www.ace.mmu.ac.uk/esd/principles/carrying_capacity.html

See also http://en.wikipedia.org/wiki/Carrying_capacity

## City Region

The term city region came into widespread use in Britain to mean something like the metropolitan area, or city-orientated conurbation around 2004, following the dropping of plans for regional assemblies in England, itself a result of the rejection of this plan in a referendum in North East England.

With the budget statement 2009 the concept gained further momentum as Manchester and Leeds were granted city region status, conferring increased economic autonomy on the inter-authority bodies - in the vase of Manchester AGMA, the Association of Greater Manchester Authorities.

See http://www.nwda.co.uk/news--events/press-releases/200901/manchester-city-region-status.aspx

http://www.nwda.co.uk/news--events/press-releases/200901/manchester-city-region-status.aspx

http://greendealmanchester.wordpress.com/2009/05/17/new-commentary-on-the-manchester-city-region-pilot-announcement/

## Contradiction

Within a particular complex system, certain elements will compete with one another, cancel each other out, or create a crisis situation that can only be resolved through some more fundamental change. In the system of capitalism, contradictions emerge that threaten its survival. Marx and Engels pointed to the contradiction between forces of production and relations of production. They also showed how the expansion of production contradicted the impoverishment of working people leading to repeated crises. Today the capitalist system produces ever more capital which has to be absorbed/recycled - similarly its over-production of consumer goods produces a contradiction in terms of the available market to absorb the goods - particularly as wages have been kept down under the neoliberal regime - hence the credit bubble and crash. Finally the dependence of the capitalist system on ever greater resource throughputs contradicts the finite scale of the planet on which we live.

For Marxian analysis then, contradictions within the system and between the system and its environment are a fundamental way of understanding its repeated crises and its eventual destruction. However a note of caution is required: capitalism has proved extremely flexible, finding a variety of 'fixes' that enabled it to overcome its contradictions.

## Crash

This is what happens after a population overshoots the capacity of its environment to support it - note that this only requires one critical limiting factor.

See Diamond, J (2006) **Collapse.** http://books.google.co.uk/books?id=QyzHKSCYSmsC&dq=diamond+collapse

## Crisis

In formal terms this means a situation wherein the contradictions of a system reach a level beyond which they cannot be contained. This leads to a reorganisation of resources, arrangements, relationships, values and so on. For example the crisis of Keynesian 'welfare capitalism' in the 1970s led to a crisis that led to the imposition of a regime of neoliberal policies, first by the Labour government and then by the Tories. This involved a curtailment of the power of organised labour, the movement of public assets into private hands (privatisation, demutualisation, etc), the conversion of some things into commodities (social care , education, public space) and hence generators of profit and the extension of the capitalist system to new areas of the globe - for example via neo-colonialism rolling back the advances made by national liberation struggles in the former empires and the eventual overstretch of the soviet socialist states leading to their collapse and entry into the capitalist global orbit.

Or we could look at he example of Peak Energy which will provoke a set of linked crises in relation to the economy as a whole, food distribution and security, transportation and human settlement, etc.

Less formally, 'crisis' refers to any situation in which a system faces a significant challenge.

## Drawdown

This is where resources needed to support life are consumed at a greater rate than they are replaced. Sound familiar?

## Edge

An ecological concept. The edge or 'ecotone' is where two ecosystems meet. This area tends to have characteristics of both ecosystems with a resulting richness of species and energy transactions. The edge concept is used extensively in permaculture as a design principle to maximise yield. It can also be applied to social systems.

See http://www.permacultureprinciples.com/principle_11.php

http://www.thepsychologist.org.uk/archive/archive_home.cfm?volumeID=20&editionID=146&ArticleID=1172

http://www.compsy.org.uk/edge.htm

## Endogenous development

Endogenous development means development from within - in this case from within the communities of the Manchester-Mersey bioregion. It must be stressed that endogenous development does mean a change of emphasis from global competition to relative regional self-reliance. It means creating, sharing and using wealth locally and not depending on inward investment - the model that became dominant during the height of neoliberal madness. The term is being used in Venezuela to describe local economic development supported by State aid.

## Energy austerity

Energy austerity means the coming times when (unless the technologists manage to make nuclear fusion, thorium reactors, algae or such like work) we will have to live on considerably less energy than we are used to. This has profound implications for the way we organise the economy and live our lives. So much of hat is taken for granted is based on massive energy inputs, most of it from hydrocarbons - food, travel, heating, lighting, telecommunications, construction, and hence the very spatial and temporal (to do with time) nature of our settlements.

See the Transition Handbook
http://www.appropedia.org/TTH:_Introduction

Post carbon Cities http://www.postcarboncities.net/

## Energy descent

Refers to a community's planned reduction of energy use, rather than waiting for a crisis. See entry for Energy austerity

See The Transition Handbook Chapter 2, section *Why Energy Descent?*
http://www.appropedia.org/TTH_Chapter_2:_The_view_from_the_mountain-top

## Energy subsidy

Refers to the idea that our current economic system is dependent on a supplementary resource in terms of large inputs of energy (mainly in the form of hydrocarbons - oil, gas, coal). Other socio-economic systems have similarly used energy subsidies - e.g. water power, human power in he form of slavery, animal power. The problem with the current situation is that the energy subsidy is not sustainable and therefore nor is the system.

## Fiscal stimulus

Government spending to re-stimulate a stagnant economy. This comes from JM Keynes' ideas on the stimulation of demand to get the economy moving again when in recession. In the 1930s this was attempted by Roosevelt's New Deal policies but actually the effective fiscal stimulus came in the form of military spending during the anti-fascist war of 1939-45. In the present recession, caused by the bursting of the credit bubble, most governments have funded some degree of fiscal stimulus, financed by running up a big debt. However much of this has gone straight into the banks (a transfer from public to private hands) and has not re-stimulated the 'real' economy. Some commentators (e.g. the New Economics Foundation and The LSE group led by Nicolas Stern have called for a Green fiscal stimulus where spending on things like a massive home insulation programme would stimulate the economy. But the catch from an ecological point of view is that this will just get us back to business as usual, the continued burning of the planet's assets beyond a sustainable (i.e. replacement) level.

## Food security

The ability of a community (family, village, town, region, country) to guarantee food for its people. In the UK we import the greater part of our food and have very low stocks of staples. Food security is therefore low despite the apparent abundance which is dependent on the continuation of supply chains. The vulnerability of these was demonstrated during the lorry driver's dispute in 2000.

See http://www.21school.ox.ac.uk/downloads/briefings/PFPShould_Britain_Feed_Itself.pdf

http://www.neweconomics.org/gen/z_sys_PublicationDetail.aspx?PID=271

http://transitionculture.org/wp-content/uploads/2007/CanBritain.pdf

## Green Deal

We use this as a catch all term for any package of ecological friendly policies and initiatives that are also characterised by an emphasis on maximising social and economic justice for all.

See http://greendealmanchester.wordpress.com/

## Green New Deal

The New Economics Foundation and others have proposed a Green New Deal which would specifically re-stimulate the present economy through ecologically friendly policies. However this approach we believe will sooner or late result in contradictions between ecology and the dynamic of capital accumulation.

See
http://www.neweconomics.org/gen/z_sys_publicationdetail.aspx?pid=258

## Keynesianism

In the years of the Great Depression of the 1930s, John Maynard Keynes proposed that in order to get the economy moving again government should put additional money into the economy. It could do this through major public expenditure programmes, financed by public debt that would be repaid as the economy boomed again. The idea was to put money back into people's pockets (reducing their tendency to save/hoard in difficult times) and thereby get production and distribution moving again. In the current recession most governments have made some degree of intervention of this sort.

The idea is of course to ameliorate the perverse functioning of the market, not to radically alter the capitalist system itself. However in the post war period increased public spending had a Keynesian demand stimulatory effect, also altering the balance (temporarily, it turned out) between capital and labour.

## Marxism

Karl Marx and Frederic Engels developed a revolutionary way to understand society. This was based on two key discoveries. Firstly the materialist basis of history - that what happens in human society is a result of the processes that produce the wherewithal to live (food, shelter, warmth and so on). It is this rather than the will of rulers, ideas and beliefs, that is fundamental, which is not to say that the role of ideas or of leaders, of politics is unimportant or insignificant. Secondly that capitalist production, growth and the creation of wealth is based on the extraction of surplus value from the worker - the theft of time and effort. Upon this base Marx and Engels developed an encompassing approach, that is still being taken forward by others, that is at once a critique of conventional economics (and social science) and a tool (not a dogma) for making sense of the world we live in, for example why economic growth is the current faith and dogma despite evidence of its environmental consequences, why there is still global poverty, why national and international agreements damage the interests of ordinary people, or why there are still wars.

Marx and Engels also emphasised the role of working people themselves in overturning capitalism and for this reason their influence has been particularly important in the international movements of workers and peasants (but much less so in the English speaking world). They were not just ivory tower scholars (Engels didn't even get to University), but practical revolutionaries - what Antonio Gramsci later called organic intellectuals, at their best expounding neither theory or practice alone, but praxis, the unity of theory and practice.

Marxism is the name given to this approach to making sense of the world. It has been linked with the socialist states of the last century but many Marxists stand outside that tradition. Marxian is a term sometimes used to describe those approaches that draw on Marx but also add other concepts and analyses.

Marxism has found new vigour in the experience of exclusion and impoverishment in the countries of the global South and of the crash that began in 2007. As Enrique Dussel put it, the second century of Marx (1983-2083) will be particularly fertile:

> *Marx in his second century will be something very different from in his first century. He will be a Marx whose critical thought will be in the hands of humanity - critical of capitalism and, in a positive way (opening its democratic and creative era), of [soviet] socialism. We are perhaps nearer to Marx than ever.*

## Peak Energy

A concept developed initially in relation to oil reserves where it noted that the critical point for an oil dependent economy was not the point at which oil reserves were exhausted but the point at which consumption outstripped the discovery of new reserves. For any oil reserve there is a peak in output after which it inexorably declines with remaining reserves progressively more difficult to extract. This relationship applies for a particular oil reserve, country, region or the world as a whole.

The same thinking can be applied to gas, coal, uranium.

Peak (non-renewable) energy is a limiting factor on any economy that does not have alternative energy supplies and/or one that squanders its energy.

See http://www.theoildrum.com/
http://www.youtube.com/watch?v=Ulxe1ie-vEY

http://www.youtube.com/watch?v=ybRz91eimTg&feature=related

## Permaculture

Originally conceived of as "permanent agriculture" but subsequently broadened to mean a design approach to human settlement and cultivation based on ecological principles. The idea is to mimic natural systems (such as a woodland ecology or forest edge) to build resilience and maximise yield. The concept was developed in Australia and not all techniques associated with permaculture (for example sheet mulching) have travelled well to other places. Nevertheless as a design approach it has great potential and an increasingly varied and mature body of practice and evidence to rest on. Moreover some classic permaculture design ideas such as the combined chicken-shed and greenhouse or the forest garden illustrate the principles in action. Emphasises necessary use, combination of functions, harvesting of natural energies and resources (e.g. rainwater, solar radiation).

See

http://attra.ncat.org/attra-pub/perma.html

http://www.holmgren.com.au/DLFiles/PDFs/EssenceofPC3.pdf

## Resilience

"Resilience is the capacity of a system to absorb disturbance and reorganise while undergoing change, so as to still retain essentially the same function, structure, identity and feedbacks."[58]

This capacity of a system (or community) depends on at least four dimensions including

1. • Diversity – the variation within the system. A field of one crop is more vulnerable to pest attack than a field of mixed crops.
2. • Modularity – the extent to which the system is broken up into relatively autonomous subsystems. The banking crash of 2008 was exacerbated by the size and interdependence of financial institutions.
3. • Tightness of Feedbacks – the speed with which the system can respond to disturbance. You are sitting in the garden and it begins to rain, so you bring in the washing before it gets wet. You are inside and don't notice it is raining until the washing is soaked. In the former case the feedback is tight.
4. • Redundancy – the extent to which the system has duplication of elements. If you are growing 1 lettuce and the slugs get it, you have no lettuce. If you have several plants you can afford to lose one.

Our economies with their monopolies, just in time supply chains and reliance on oil inputs are not resilient – "nine meals from anarchy".

See
http://www.appropedia.org/TTH_Chapter_3:_Why_rebuilding_resilience_is_as_important_as_cutting_carbon_emissions

## Shock proofing

The process of building resilience to reasonably foreseeable shocks and threats. For example, strengthening flood defences, increasing the capacity of local communities to grow and store food. So far the emphasis of public authorities has been more on strengthening crisis management systems (for example in the event of a terrorist strike, or a pandemic) but not to increase the resilience of the community and its economy as a means of reducing vulnerability to the shock.

Both resilience and shock proofing as understood here stand somewhere between the mitigation and adaptation strategies for preventing and responding to (for example) climate change.

## Strategic localism

It is necessary in a post carbon world to live our lives more locally. It will be necessary to source many more things locally, to travel less, to make our horizons more local. But this is not going to be a total localisation, returning to a village scale. Strategic localism recognises that the bioregional scale is the appropriate one for organising an economy in a post carbon world. It rejects parochialism and is internationalist in perspective, yet it is localist because of the need to live on a smaller scale, from a smaller footprint. It is strategic because it prioritises the degree of localness according to the need, the scarcity of the product, the appropriate scale of organisation. It is a corollary of trade subsidiarity.

## Trade subsidiarity

Because of the imperatives of reducing energy expenditure and (re)generating a real local economy it is at the regional level that transformative green strategies can make the most sense. It is unsustainable to import our food and our sources of wealth from outside the region. Some needs will have to be met from imports and trade but a principle of subsidiarity needs to be applied - only bring in those things that are both necessary and cannot be sourced or made locally. There will of course still be relationships with other parts of the world. These will involve necessary trade, sharing of knowledge and solidarity. Moreover in our relatively fortunate situation we have an ongoing responsibility to some producers as a result of the distortion of agriculture and other production over the years of colonial and postcolonial domination - thus Windward Island bananas might still be imported (by hi-tech sailing ship?) while aid is given to enable that bioregion to endogenously develop in its own right.

See P. A. Kropotkin, *Fields, factories, and workshops; or, Industry combined with agriculture and brain work with manual work* (New, rev., and enl. ed.). New York and London,: Thomas Nelson & Sons, 1912.

## Transition

Moving from one state to another. But here we mean the managed process of moving from the hydrocarbon-dependent, productivist-consumptionist current system to one where we live within the resources of the planet. There is a growing movement that uses a concept akin to this to plan for transition to low carbon living in particular towns, cities, neighbourhoods. The Green Deal for the Manchester-Mersey Bioregion is a transition approach at the bioregional level.

See http://transitiontowns.org/Main.HomePage
http://www.appropedia.org/The_Transition_Handbook_-_free_edit_version

## Watershed

The area of land that drains its water into a particular river system the catchment of the river system.

Thus the Mersey watershed includes the West face of the Pennines between behind Rochdale and Congleton and the various tributaries that join the estuary (Roch, Irk, Medlock, Dane, Bollin, Weaver, and so on). But the watershed is more than the rivers - it is the land around them. Watersheds often define the boundaries of a bioregion.

# Notes

[1] This is a further development of a brief discussion paper: "We need a new model of economic development" first published at http://greendealmanchester.wordpress.com/ in 2009. I am grateful to participants at the Call to Real Action concrete Utopias workshop on steady state economics for stimulating some of the ideas presented here.

[2] The immediate context for this discussion was reflection on dominant discourses within the North West Region and in particular the background papers for the North West Regional Development Agency's forthcoming Regional Strategy http://www.nwregionalstrategy.com/home. However, the assumptions are not unique to the North West and are indeed pervasive across the world in general.

[3] While of general relevance the context for the discussion of an alternative approach is the North West of England and specifically the Manchester-Mersey Bioregion. See http://greendealmanchester.wordpress.com/the-manchester-bioregion/

[4] The critique of economic growth goes back at least to the report Limits to Growth (Meadows et al.) in 1972. Arguments against regional specialisation were persuasively made by Kropotkin in his book of 1912, Fields, Factories and Workshops.

[5] http://www.tradingeconomics.com/Economics/GDP-Growth.aspx?Symbol=GBP The comparable international rates are 3.2% (21 years to double)for the advanced economies and 5.0% (14 years to double) for the rest (IMF members only) International Monetary Fund, World Economic Outlook Database, October 2008, cited by Manchester Independent Economic review http://www.manchester-review.org.uk/download/?id=549

[6] Prosperity Without Growth: The transition to a Sustainable Economy. Tim Jackson Sustainable Development Commission http://www.sd-commission.org.uk/publications/downloads/prosperity_without_growth_report.pdf

[7] http://www.footprintnetwork.org/en/index.php/GFN/page/trends/uk/

[8] http://www.footprintnetwork.org/en/index.php/GFN/page/world_footprint/

[9] Jackson, T (2009) Prosperity Without Growth - see note 6.

[10] http://neweconomics.org/publications/growth-isn%E2%80%99t-working

[11] see S Mehrota and E Delamonica "Eliminating Human Poverty: Macroeconomic and social policies for equitable growth." London, Zed, 2007. Review: http://tinyurl.com/3a53cdj

[12] See my "Sustainability: Utopian and Scientific" at http://greendealmanchester.wordpress.com/

[13] Some of the ideas presented here are explored at greater length in my pamphlet *A Green Deal for the Manchester-Mersey Bioregion* http://greendealmanchester.wordpress.com/

[14] Some of the words used are explored in the bioregional glossary at http://greendealmanchester.wordpress.com/concepts-for-bioregional-development/

[15] In Venezuela, where the term is being used widely, it also refers to community based production products pump-primed by generous State investment.

[16] Green Books (2002)

[17] Maquiladora - a factory, classically just inside Mexico's northern border where global capitalists or their local subcontractors exploit the lower costs (less regulation, low wages) of production in a 'developing' country.

[18] Raymond Williams, widely regarded as the UK's leading socialist intellectual of the latter half of the 20th Century, emphasised this aspect of working class culture and consistently but fruitlessly called for its incorporation in the vision and policy of the socialist movement. As he acknowledged, his consciousness of this way of living, this ordinary culture, had its roots in his upbringing in socialist and trades-unionist family in a Welsh Border village. See http://en.wikipedia.org/wiki/Raymond_Williams and http://www.robertchristgau.com/xg/bkrev/williams-85.php for introductions to his work.

[19] http://inclusiveandsustainable.ning.com/forum/topics/sustainable-inclusive

[20] The participatory budgeting developed in Workers Party run local authorities in Brazil is one example of what can be done,(see http://en.wikipedia.org/wiki/Participatory_budgeting and Santos, Boaventura de Sousa (1998), Participatory Budgeting in Porto Alegre: Toward a Redistributive Democracy, *Politics & Society*, 26, 4, 461-510 http://www.boaventuradesousasantos.pt/media/pdfs/Participatory_Budgeting_Politics_and_Society_1998.PDF . but this only extends to the local authority's budget - not to the rest of the economy. Michael Albert's participatory economics suggests some ways such an economy might be organised, but alas without any clear praxis or theory of how this can be attained. His economics is also pretty illiterate - look in vain for 'accumulation', 'surplus value', growth, and he says some silly things about the bioregionalist approach http://www.zcommunications.org/zparecon/pareconlac.htm .

Pat Devine's *Democracy and Democratic Planning* Cambridge: Polity Press, 1988 (but recently reprinted with a new preface) gives a more adequate treatment of the issues although the model is still rather abstract. Readers of Spanish will find a detailed summary at http://www.rebelion.org/docs/97087.pdf. For shorter discussions see P Devine, Social ownership and democratic planning. In P Devine, A Pearmain and D Purdy eds. (2009) *Feelbad Britain: how to make it better.* London: Lawrence and Wishart (http://www.lwbooks.co.uk/books/archive/feelbad_britain.html).

[21] The experience of the Cuban economy is instructive here - the State mobilised the people and also used selective foreign investment, for example to exploit nickel reserves and develop tourism when the soviet subsidy for the economy collapsed in the early 1990s. See http://www.cubasol-manch.org.uk/Changes%20in%20Cuba.html

[22] The SDC paper cited above (9) begins the task of developing a macro-economics of a no growth economy.

[23] http://neweconomics.org/publications/nine-meals-anarchy

[23] Because I have seen not evidence that this has happened anywhere - these schemes, even in the context of official currency meltdown, as in Argentina, seem to remain on the margins.

[23] These contradictions include the tendency of the rate of profit to fall with technical innovation, the over-capacity of the productive forces (in relation to consumption, particularly as at the same time there is a drive to keep wages down) and the problem of absorbing and re-investing ever growing capital.

[24] To use a rather 1970s term.

[25] Two working class districts in the city of Manchester..

[26] Because I have seen no evidence that this has happened anywhere - these schemes, even in the context of official currency meltdown, as in Argentina, seem to remain on the margins.

[27] QANGOs: Quasi autonomous non-governmental organisations - such as the North West Development Agency, or the Primary Care Trusts.

[28] These contradictions include the tendency of the rate of profit to fall with technical innovation, the over-capacity of the productive forces (in relation to consumption, particularly as at the same time there is a drive to keep wages down) and the problem of absorbing and re-investing ever growing capital.

[29] These come from various sources. The New Economics Foundation is a particularly important producer of such material.

[30] Originally published in 1877 as part of Anti-Dühring (http://www.marxists.org/archive/marx/works/1877/anti-duhring/index.htm), published as a separate pamphlet 1892 http://www.marxists.org/archive/marx/works/1880/soc-utop/index.htm .

[31] The critique of economic growth goes back at least to the report Limits to Growth (Meadows et al.) in 1972.

[32] http://www.tradingeconomics.com/Economics/GDP-Growth.aspx?Symbol=GBP The comparable international rates are 3.2% (21 years to double)for the advanced economies and 5.0% (14 years to double) for the rest (IMF members only) International Monetary Fund, World Economic Outlook Database, October 2008, cited by Manchester Independent Economic review http://www.manchester-review.org.uk/download/?id=549

[33] Prosperity Without Growth: The transition to a Sustainable Economy. Tim Jackson Sustainable Development Commission http://www.sd-commission.org.uk/publications/downloads/prosperity_without_growth_report.pdf

[34] http://www.footprintnetwork.org/en/index.php/GFN/page/trends/uk/

[35] http://www.footprintnetwork.org/en/index.php/GFN/page/world_footprint/

[36] Jackson, T (2009) Prosperity Without Growth: The transition to a Sustainable Economy. London: Sustainable Development Commission http://www.sd-commission.org.uk/publications/downloads/prosperity_without_growth_report.pdf.

[37] New Economics Foundation, A Green New Deal. Joined-up policies to solve the triple crunch of the credit crisis, climate change and high oil prices: The first report of the Green New Deal Group, 2008.

[38] The Happy Planet Index 2.0: Why good lives don't have to cost the Earth: http://www.neweconomics.org/gen/z_sys_publicationdetail.aspx?pid=289

National Accounts of Well-being: bringing real wealth onto the balance sheet http://www.neweconomics.org/gen/z_sys_publicationdetail.aspx?pid=268

A Green New Deal: Joined-up policies to solve the triple crunch of the credit crisis, climate change and high oil prices http://www.neweconomics.org/gen/z_sys_publicationdetail.aspx?pid=258

[39] The Fabian society, established at the end of the 19th Century took its name from the Roman general Quintus Fabius Maximus whose tactics of repeated guerrilla type assaults on the invading Carthaginians were ultimately successful. The Fabians sought a reformist path to socialism, eschewing class struggle. Their approach has tended to be based on presenting ideas and proposals, often backed with social scientific research in

order to convince those in positions of power, a style of engagement identical to that of NEF, the SDC and other similar lobby groups.

[40] This is perhaps a little unfair in the case of the SDC - in their report *Prosperity Without Growth* Jackson does offer the beginnings of an analysis of the appropriate macro economics of a no-growth economy. The problem is there is no analysis of what might bring this about, either in terms of the contradictions of the present system or of the social forces that could be recruited to the struggle for such an approach.

[41] The distinction is from Gramsci. See page 22.

[42] Capital (with a capital 'C') refers here to a cohesive subsystem in society comprised of both capital in economic terms *and* the actions, strategy, ideology of those who work to increase the accumulation of capital - its production and reproduction and expansion. These people were initially the classical industrial capitalists of the 19th Century, but over the last 100 years the function has been to greater or lesser extent become systemic in nature, with the development of professions such as accountancy and the establishment of bodies such as pension funds and corporate bonds that function objectively as the capitalist.

[43] E.g. Abdallah S, Thompson S, Michaelson J, Marks N and Steuer N (2009) The (un)Happy Planet Index 2.0. Why good lives don't have to cost the Earth (NEF: London)

[44] Ref to Wilkinson and the equality website

[45] The SDC report (see note 33) (Chapter 6) sets out a version of this cycle but sanitises the elements - referring to investment and profit rather than capital, for example.

[46] Engels, F. (1892/1970) Socialism: Utopian and Scientific. Moscow: Progress Publishers edition, p. 57.

[47] "Here is a conclusion I've come to after many years: among all the errors we may have committed, the greatest of them all was that we believed that someone really knew something about socialism, or that someone actually knew how to build socialism". Speech delivered by Dr. Fidel Castro Ruz, President of the Republic of Cuba, at the Commemoration of the 60th Anniversary of his admission to University of Havana, in the Aula Magna of the University of Havana, on November 17, 2005. http://www.cuba.cu/gobierno/discursos/2005/ing/f171105i.html .

[48] Socialism: Utopian and Scientific (see note 46) p. 72.

[49] What closely links Marx's theory with scientific thought is the rational understanding of the forces which really operate in society. But Marx's theory is fundamentally beyond scientific thought, and it preserves scientific thought only by superseding it: what is in question is an understanding of struggle, and not of law. "We know only one science: the science of history" (Marx and Engels: The German Ideology).

[50] For a good introduction see http://www.hegemonics.co.uk/gramsci.html

[51] Margaret Thatcher – TINA.

[52] To use the Trotskyist term – which does not mean that we are either calling the SDC a bunch of Trots, nor endorsing Trotskyist politics in general.

[53] Chapter 8, see note 9.

[54] Jackson, see note 33, pp 78–79.

[55] Victor, Peter 2008b Managing without Growth. Thinkpiece for the SDC workshop 'Confronting Structure'. April 2008. London: Sustainable Development Commission. Online at: http://www.sd-commission.org.uk/publications/downloads/Peter_Victor_thinkpiece.pdf

[56] Rather interestingly this is a quotation from Ed Miliband, UK Secretary of State for Climate, December 2008 (quoted without citation in Prosperity Without Growth, p 98 see note 33.

[57] There is an important point behind this wider meaning – competence is not a property of an individual person but something shared between the individual and their social context – the culture makes us competent. Elsewhere we call this 'social capability', see http://openlibrary.org/b/OL10184601M/Social-Skills-for-People-With-Learning-Disabilities

[58] Walker, B, Hollinger, C.S., Carpenter, S.R. and Kinzig, A. (2004) 'Resilience, Adaptability and Transformability in Social-ecological Systems', *Ecology and Society* 9 (2) p.5. cited at http://www.appropedia.org/TTH_Chapter_3:_Why_rebuilding_resilience_is_as_important_as_cutting_carbon_emissions